Portuguese Desserts

15 Mouth-Watering Portuguese Desserts

CONTENTS

Introduction

Welcome to the delightful world of Portuguese desserts! From creamy custard tarts to indulgent chocolate cakes, this book is a celebration of the mouthwatering sweet treats that Portugal has to offer. In this enchanting journey, we will explore the rich culinary heritage of Portugal, uncovering the secrets behind its beloved desserts. Whether you have a sweet tooth or simply appreciate the art of baking, this book is your ultimate guide to mastering the art of Portuguese desserts. So, grab your apron, preheat that oven, and get ready to immerse yourself in the irresistible flavors of Portugal. Let's embark on this delectable adventure together!

Recipe 1

Portuguese Custard Tarts

12 servings   🕐 2 hrs 35 mins

Portuguese custard tarts (or pasteis de nata) are crisp, creamy, and decadently sweet. This Portuguese dessert recipe features a delicately spiced flavor and uses pantry ingredients like egg yolks, flour, and cinnamon to create a one-of-a-kind pastry.

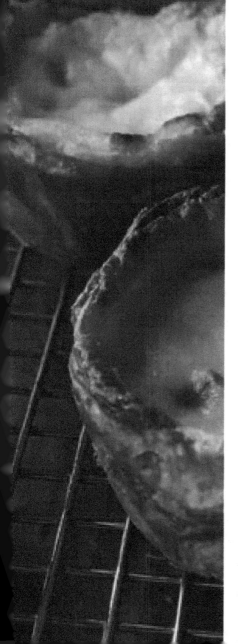

Ingredients

Dough:
- 1 cup all-purpose flour
- ¼ teaspoon kosher salt
- ⅓ cup cold water
- 1 stick high-quality unsalted butter, fully softened, divided

Sugar Syrup:
- ¾ cup white sugar
- ¼ cup water
- 1 tablespoon water
- 1 cinnamon stick (Optional)
- 1 lemon, zested in large strips (Optional)

Custard Base:
- ⅓ cup all-purpose flour
- ¼ teaspoon kosher salt
- 1 ½ cups milk
- 6 large egg yolks
- 1 teaspoon vanilla extract (Optional)

Portuguese Custard Tarts

12 servings   🕐 2 hrs 35 mins

Portuguese custard tarts (or pasteis de nata) are crisp, creamy, and decadently sweet. This Portuguese dessert recipe features a delicately spiced flavor and uses pantry ingredients like egg yolks, flour, and cinnamon to create a one-of-a-kind pastry.

Method

Step 1: Combine flour, salt, and cold water in a bowl. Mix with a wooden spoon until dough just comes together and pulls away from the sides of the bowl. Dough should be sticky; adjust with more flour or water to achieve

Step 2: Transfer dough onto a well-floured surface. Dust a little more flou over the top. Knead for 1 to 2 minutes to form a round. Cover and let rest for 15 to 20 minutes.

Step 3: Roll dough into a square about 1/8-inch-thick, dusting with flour as necessary; dough should still be sticky

Step 4: Spread 1/3 of the butter over 2 of the square using a silicone spatula, leaving a 1/2-inch border. Flip the unbuttered side over the middle of th square and fold the opposite end over like a letter. Straighten the edges as needed.

4

Portuguese Custard Tarts

12 servings   🕐 2 hrs 35 mins

Portuguese custard tarts (or pasteis de nata) are crisp, creamy, and decadently sweet. This Portuguese dessert recipe features a delicately spiced flavor and uses pantry ingredients like egg yolks, flour, and cinnamon to create a one-of-a-kind pastry.

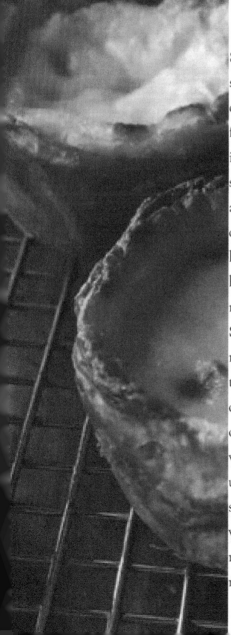

Method

Step 5: Turn dough with a bench scraper to unstick it from the counter; dust with flour. Flip and sprinkle more flour on top. Roll dough into a 1/8-inch-thick rectangle, carefully stretching edges as needed. Spread another 1/3 of the butter over 2/3 of the dough. Fold into thirds. Transfer onto a lined baking sheet and freeze until butter is slightly chilled, about 10 minutes.

Step 6: Sprinkle dough with flour and roll into a square a little over 1/8-inch-thick. Spread remaining butter over the dough, leaving a 1- to 1 1/2-inch border on the top edge. Dip your finger in water and lightly moisten the unbuttered edge. Roll dough into a log starting from the bottom edge. Dust with more flour and polish the ends as needed. Seal with plastic wrap and refrigerate at least 2 hours.

Portuguese Custard Tarts

12 servings   🕐 2 hrs 35 mins

Portuguese custard tarts (or pasteis de nata) are crisp, creamy, and decadently sweet. This Portuguese dessert recipe features a delicately spiced flavor and uses pantry ingredients like egg yolks, flour, and cinnamon to create a one-of-a-kind pastry.

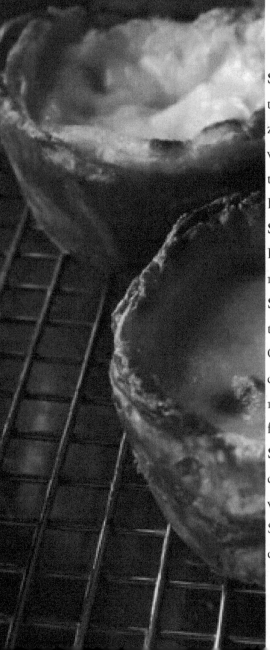

Method

Step 7: Combine sugar, 1/4 cup plus 1 tablespoon water, cinnamon, and lemon zest in a pot. Boil over medium heat, without stirring, until syrup reaches 210 to 215 degrees F (100 degrees C). Remove from heat.

Step 8: Preheat the oven to 550 degrees F (288 degrees C). Grease a 12-cup muffin tin.

Step 9: Whisk flour, salt, and cold milk together very thoroughly in a cold pot. Cook over medium heat, whisking constantly, until milk thickens, about minutes. Remove from heat and let cool for at least 10 minutes.

Step 10: Whisk egg yolks into the cooled milk. Add sugar syrup and vanilla extract. Mix until combined. Strain custard into a glass measuring cup.

Portuguese Custard Tarts

12 servings   🕐 2 hrs 35 mins

Portuguese custard tarts (or pasteis de nata) are crisp, creamy, and decadently sweet. This Portuguese dessert recipe features a delicately spiced flavor and uses pantry ingredients like egg yolks, flour, and cinnamon to create a one-of-a-kind pastry.

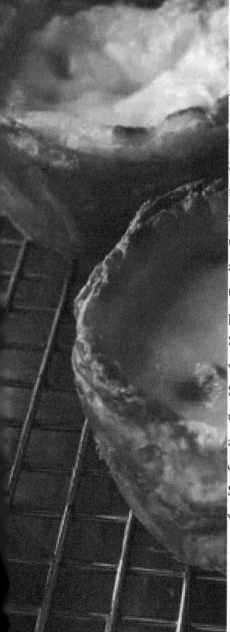

Method

Step 11: Unwrap the dough and trim any uneven bits on the ends. Score log into 12 even pieces using a knife; cut through.

Step 12: Place a piece of dough in each muffin cup. Dip your thumb lightly in some cold water. Press your thumb into the center of the swirl; push dough against the bottom and up the sides of the cup until it reaches least 1/8 inch past the top.

Step 13: Fill each cup 3/4 of the way with custard.

Step 14: Bake in the preheated oven until the pastry is browned and bubbly, and the tops start to blister and caramelize, about 12 minutes.

Step 15: Cool tarts briefly and serve warm. Enjoy!

Recipe 2

Serradura

4 servings   🕐 5 hrs 20 mins

Portuguese custard tarts (or pasteis de nata) are crisp, creamy, and decadently sweet. This Portuguese dessert recipe features a delicately spiced flavor and uses pantry ingredients like egg yolks, flour, and cinnamon to create a one-of-a-kind pastry.

Ingredients

Measuring cup used, 1 Cup = 250 ml, 1 tsp = 5 ml

1/2 pint / 1 cup heavy whipping cream

1/4 cup sweetened condensed milk, adjust as per desired sweetness

1/2 tsp vanilla extract

16-18 Marie biscuits

Cherries/chocolate shavings, for garnishing, as required

Serradura

4 servings   🕐 5 hrs 20 mins

Portuguese custard tarts (or pasteis de nata) are crisp, creamy, and decadently sweet. This Portuguese dessert recipe features a delicately spiced flavor and uses pantry ingredients like egg yolks, flour, and cinnamon to create a one-of-a-kind pastry.

Method

Step 1: Transfer the Marie biscuits into a food processor/blender and make a fine powder that almost looks like sawdust.

Step 2: In the bowl of your stand mixer fitted with a whisk attachment/ or use hand blender, add in the chilled heavy cream, beat on medium-high speed until it forms soft peaks.

Step 3: Now add in the condensed milk along with the vanilla extract and beat until it forms stiff peak. Do not overbeat or else you will end up with butter.

Serradura

4 servings   🕐 5 hrs 20 mins

Portuguese custard tarts (or pasteis de nata) are crisp, creamy, and decadently sweet. This Portuguese dessert recipe features a delicately spiced flavor and uses pantry ingredients like egg yolks, flour, and cinnamon to create a one-of-a-kind pastry.

Method

Step 4: Assembling the pudding- Spoon the whipped cream mixture in a serving glass (You may use a piping bag like I did, for a neater finish), then top with the crushed Marie biscuit powder, continue layering with the cream and Marie biscuit powder, ending with the cream layer. Sprinkle some of the crushed Marie biscuit powder on top, and refrigerate it for about 4-6 hours so that it sets well. Garnish with cherries or chocolate shavings and serve chilled.

Recipe 3

Portuguese sponge cake

12 servings   🕐 1 hr 15 mins

Pão de ló is one of the most popular cakes in Portugal. This simple light and spongy cake dates back to the 1700s. It's a perfect companion to an evening coffee or tea.

Ingredients

Cake

- 1 + 1/2 cups sugar
- 7 large eggs whites and yolks separated, at room temperature
- 1/4 cup water at room temperature
- 1/4 cup freshly squeezed lemon juice
- 1 1/2 tbsp lemon zest
- 1 1/2 cups all purpose flour
- 1/2 tsp salt
- 1/2 tsp creme of tarter

Strawberry topping

- ¼ cup water
- 1 tbs cornstarch
- ½ cup sugar
- 2 tsp freshly squeezed lemon juice
- 4 cups strawberries , hulled and sliced

13

Portuguese sponge cake

12 servings   🕐 1 hr 15 mins

Pão de ló is one of the most popular cakes in Portugal. This simple light and spongy cake dates back to the 1700s. It's a perfect companion to an evening coffee or tea.

Method

Cake

Step 1: Pre-heat the oven to 350 °F

Step 2: In a stand mixer, beat the egg yolks and 1 cup of sugar, on medium high until light and fluffy.

Step 3: Reduce the stand mixer to medium speed and add the water, lemon juice and lemon zest. Mix until well combined.

Step 4: Sift the flour and salt together into a large bowl.

Step 5: Pour the yolk mixture over the flour, whisk together and set aside.

Step 6: In a clean stand mixer bowl, add the egg whites and beat on medium high.

Step 7: Add the cream of tarter after about 1 minute.

Portuguese sponge cake

12 servings 🕐 1 hr 15 mins

Pão de ló is one of the most popular cakes in Portugal. This simple light and spongy cake dates back to the 1700s. It's a perfect companion to an evening coffee or tea.

Method

Step 8: Once the egg whites start to form soft peaks, slowly pour in the remaining 1/2 cup of sugar while continuing to beat.

Step 9: Keep beating until stiff peaks form. To test this, remove the stand mixer whisk. Peaks should stand without tipping over. This can take about 5 minutes.

Step 10: Add the egg whites to the remaining ingredients and fold in with a rubber spatula until well combined.

Note: Do not over mix or beat the ingredients during this step.

Step 11: Run cold water inside of the tube pan with cold water and let it drip out.

Step 12: Pour the batter into the tube pan and place the pan in the oven on the middle rack.

Portuguese sponge cake

12 servings   🕐 1 hr 15 mins

Pão de ló is one of the most popular cakes in Portugal. This simple light and spongy cake dates back to the 1700s. It's a perfect companion to an evening coffee or tea.

Method

Step 13: Bake for 55 minutes or until a cake tester (or toothpick) comes out clean.

Step 14: Place the cake pan upside dow on a heat resistant surface and let cool for about 30 minutes.

Step 15: Carefully run a sharp knife around the edges of the cake.

Step 16: You should be able to pull the tube and cake out from inside the pan

Step 17: Carefully run a sharp knife between the cake bottom and the pan bottom to loosen the cake from the pa

Step 18: Lift the cake and place it on a cake plate or platter.

Step 19: Let the cake finish cooling.

Portuguese sponge cake

12 servings 🕐 1 hr 15 mins

Pão de ló is one of the most popular cakes in Portugal. This simple light and spongy cake dates back to the 1700s. It's a perfect companion to an evening coffee or tea.

Method

Strawberry topping

Step 1: Add the water and cornstarch to a medium pot.

Step 2: Whisk the cornstarch until it dissolves in the water.

Step 3: Add the sugar and turn on the heat up to medium high.

Step 4: After one minute, add the strawberries and lemon juice, and stir to combine all ingredients.

Step 5: Once the mix starts to boil, reduce the heat to medium low and cover.

Step 6: Let simmer for 10 minutes, stir every 3 or so minutes.

Step 7: Uncover and shut off the heat.

Step 8: Let cool down. The compote will thicken a bit.

Step 9: Serve warm or cold on slices of the sponge cake. And enjoy!

Recipe 4

Chocolate Salami

20 servings 🕐 3 hrs 15 mins

This Chocolate Salami recipe is a fun, no-bake Italian sweet. It's a crunchy treat that is perfect to serve with an after-dinner coffee.

Ingredients

2 cups coarsely crushed sweet cookies (chocolate chip, graham crackers, butter cookies, plain sweet cookies, digestive biscuits, vanilla wafers)

1⅓ cups coarsely crushed Amaretti cookies

⅓ cup chopped toasted almonds

½ cup cocoa powder

1 cup powdered (icing) sugar sieved

⅓ cup sweet marsala wine

10 tablespoons (1 ¼ sticks or 150 grams) butter melted

⅔ cup (4 oz or 100 grams) dark chocolate melted

Chocolate Salami

20 servings 🕐 3 hrs 15 mins

This Chocolate Salami recipe is a fun, no-bake Italian sweet. It's a crunchy treat that is perfect to serve with after-dinner coffee.

Method

Step 1: Place the dry ingredients in a medium bowl and mix well.

Step 2: In a large jug, whisk together t[...] Marsala, melted butter and melted chocolate.

Step 3: Stir wet ingredients into the d[...] ingredients.

Step 4: Prepare two lengths of double[...] plastic wrap.

Step 5: Divide the mixture between th[...] two sheets of plastic wrap and spread out into a line. Roll it up tightly into a log pressing to form the shape. Twist the end of the plastic to seal.

Step 6: Place on a baking tray (so they keep their shape) and refrigerate for a few hours.

Chocolate Salami

20 servings   🕐 3 hrs 15 mins

This Chocolate Salami recipe is a fun, no-bake Italian sweet. It's a crunchy treat that is perfect to serve with an after-dinner coffee.

Method

Step 7: After 30 minutes, check if they are still keeping the shape. If not press into shape and retighten the twists on the ends.

Step 8: Refrigerate for 3 hours or overnight.

Step 9: Or freeze if you are keeping it for some time.

Step 10: When you are ready to serve. Remove the wrapping. You can dust the salamis lightly with sifted powdered (icing) sugar to resemble the skin of the salami.

Step 11: Slice and serve. Keep it chilled to retain the shape.

Recipe 5

Portuguese Biscoitos

8 servings   🕐 38 mins

This recipe is for the Azorean Biscoitos ring-shaped biscuits that are the perfect balance of crunchy and sweet with a hint of lemon.

Ingredients

8 tablespoons unsalted butter

¾ cup granulated sugar

2 ½ cups all-purpose flour

1 teaspoon baking powder

3 large fresh eggs

4 tablespoons whole milk

½ teaspoon salt

1 teaspoon vanilla extract

1/2 teaspoon lemon zest or extract

Equipment

Standmixer with paddle attachment

oven

Large Baking Sheet

parchment paper

Portuguese Biscoitos

8 servings   🕐 38 mins

This recipe is for the Azorean Biscoitos ring-shaped biscuits that are the perfect balance of crunchy and sweet with a hint of lemon.

Method

Step 1: Preheat oven to 350° F. Line a large baking sheet with parchment paper, and lightly flour a clean cutting board or work surface.

Step 2: In the bowl of a standmixer, add the butter, and sugar. Cream until light and fluffy.

Step 3: Whisk the flour, salt, and baking powder; set aside. Add the eggs, extracts, and milk and mix until combined.

Step 4: Turn down the mixer speed and slowly add the dry ingredients into the wet ingredients. The dough should form a ball on the paddle. If it is too dry add 1 tablespoon of additional milk. If it is overly stick add one tablespoon of flour until it is workable.

Portuguese Biscoitos

8 servings   🕐 38 mins

This recipe is for the Azorean Biscoitos ring-shaped biscuits that are the perfect balance of crunchy and sweet with a hint of lemon.

Method

Step 5: Remove the dough from the stand mixer and knead on the floured workspace. The dough should be the consistency of play dough.

Step 6: I used a tablespoon-sized cookie scoop to scoop out tablespoon-sized balls.

Step 7: On the floured work space, roll on dough with the palms of your hand to create a 5 inch "snake". Bring together the ends to form a ring. Place cookies 1 inch apart of the baking sheet.

Step 8: These cookies bake for 18-20 minutes to get toasty deep golden-brown bottoms and tan golden-brown top surfaces. *See images

Step 9: Cool cookies for ten minutes before removing and baking the next batch. Repeat the process until all cookies are done.

Portuguese Biscoitos

8 servings 🕐 38 mins

This recipe is for the Azorean Biscoitos ring-shaped biscuits that are the perfect balance of crunchy and sweet with a hint of lemon.

Method

Step 10: Cooled cookies can be stored in an airtight container for up to 2 weeks time.

Notes

Nutritional values may vary and are meant to be a guide.

Recipe 6

Brazilian Carrot Cake

8 servings   🕐 1 hr

Brazilian Carrot Cake prepared in the kitchen blender and topped with milk chocolate sauce. A kid-friendly cake that also comes with useful tips for a moist cake.

Ingredients

For the cake batter:

- 17.5 oz carrots peeled and coarsely chopped
- 1 cup vegetable oil
- 1 tablespoon pure vanilla extract
- 3 large eggs at room temperature
- 1 large egg yolk
- 2 cups sugar
- 2 ⅛ cups all-purpose flour around ounces or 260 g
- 2 teaspoon baking powder
- pinch of salt

For the chocolate sauce:

- ½ cup milk chocolate chips another type of chocolate will overpower the cake
- 1 cup milk
- 2 teaspoon cornstarch dissolved i teaspoon water
- 1 tablespoon unsalted butter
- 1 tablespoon honey
- 1 tablespoon pure vanilla extract

Brazilian Carrot Cake

8 servings 1 hr

Brazilian Carrot Cake prepared in the kitchen blender and topped with milk chocolate sauce. A kid-friendly cake that also comes with useful tips for a moist cake.

Method

Step 1: Preheat oven to 350 degrees F (about 180 degrees C). Grease a round ring mold (9-inch or 23 cm diameter) and dust with flour. Remove excess flour!

Step 2: In a blender, blend the carrot, oil, vanilla, eggs and yolk, and half of the sugar together very well until the mixture is homogeneous and smooth. You may have to stop the blender more than once and scrape down the sides. Reserve.

Step 3: There are 2 ways to make this Brazilian carrot cake, depending on the texture that you choose: either super moist and dense, or slightly moist and fluffy.

Step 4: Prepare the cake batter according to one of the desired textures:

Brazilian Carrot Cake

8 servings 1 hr

Brazilian Carrot Cake prepared in the kitchen blender and topped with milk chocolate sauce. A kid-friendly cake that also comes with useful tips for a moist cake.

Method

Step 5: For a moist and dense cake (more common in Brazil): Add all the other batter ingredients (other half of the sugar, flour, baking powder, and salt) to the blended carrot mixture and blend just enough to obtain a homogeneous mixture. Youmay have to stop the blender and scrape the sides more than once). Pour into the prepared pan and bake for about 40-55 minutes. The cake is ready when a toothpick inserted in the center of the cake comes out clean.

Step 6: Let pan cool over a rack completely, slide a knife around the edges to loosen, and invert on a platter Top with the chocolate sauce (recipe below)!

Brazilian Carrot Cake

8 servings 1 hr

Brazilian Carrot Cake prepared in the kitchen blender and topped with milk chocolate sauce. A kid-friendly cake that also comes with useful tips for a moist cake.

Method

Step 7: For a fluffy cake: Pour the blended carrot mixture into a large bowl. Then, add the other half of the sugar and sift the flour and baking powder in. Add a pinch of salt and either mixture everything very well using a spatula or whisk or beat on low speed until the flour has been incorporated to the batter. Please, do not overbeat!!!

Step 8: Pour batter into the prepared pan. Bake for about 40-45 minutes or until a toothpick inserted in the center comes out clean. Yes, it will bake a little faster than when completely blended in the blender.

Step 9: Let cool completely on a wire rack. Slice a knife around the edges to loosen, unmold, and top with chocolate sauce. Decorate as desired.

31

Brazilian Carrot Cake

8 servings 1 hr

Brazilian Carrot Cake prepared in the kitchen blender and topped with milk chocolate sauce. A kid-friendly cake that also comes with useful tips for a moist cake.

Method

Step 10: You can also serve this cake plain or dusted with powdered sugar instead of topping with chocolate sauce

Step 11: This cake is moist without being oily!!! If you are intolerant of dairy, serve cake dusted with powdered sugar. To make this cake gluten-free, use a gluten-free all purpose flour (the same amount).

Step 12: To prepare the chocolate sauce In a saucepan, combine all the ingredients for the chocolate sauce, except the cornstarch and the vanilla, and cook over medium-high heat, whisking constantly. The chocolate must melt completely.

Step 13: When it starts to boil, lower the heat to medium-low and simmer until sauce has reduced and thickened little bit, about 3 minutes.

Brazilian Carrot Cake

8 servings 1 hr

Brazilian Carrot Cake prepared in the kitchen blender and topped with milk chocolate sauce. A kid-friendly cake that also comes with useful tips for a moist cake.

Method

Step 14: In a small bowl, combine the cornstarch in water until combined and not lumpy anymore. Add to the chocolate mixture and whisk until fully combined and the sauce has thickened, about 2 minutes.

Step 15: Remove from heat, stir in the vanilla extract, and let sauce cool down to warm. Pour over cake.

Step 16: To decorate (optional): If you'd like to decorate your cake with carrot rosettes, peel half of a carrot and cut thin shaves in the mandolin or with a large vegetable peeler. Then place them in a medium bowl filled with water (enough to cover the carrot shaves) and microwave on high for about 2-3 minutes or until soft.

Brazilian Carrot Cake

8 servings   1 hr

Brazilian Carrot Cake prepared in the kitchen blender and topped with milk chocolate sauce. A kid-friendly cake that also comes with useful tips for a moist cake.

Method

Step 17: Remove from the bowl and place into another bowl filled with ice water (enough to cover the shaves). Let sit for about 60 seconds and pat dry. Then, cut in half lengthwise to make less wide strips using a pairing knife and roll them like a tight curl. I also used rosemary sprigs as a garnish.

Recipe 7

Bolo Nega Maluca

6 servings   🕐 45 mins

This Brazilian Chocolate cake is easy and quick to prepare. A great everyday cake, that is also perfect for celebrations when topped with sweet brigadeiro.

Ingredients

For the Cake:

- 1/2 cup of oil
- 1 cup of sugar
- 3 eggs
- 2 cups of all purpose flour sifted
- 1 tsp of salt
- 2 tsp of baking powder
- 1 cup of chocolate powder such as Nescau or Nesquik
- 1 cup of hot water

For the Brigadeiro:

- 1 can of sweet condensed milk
- 1/2 cup of chocolate powder such as Nescau or Nesquik

Bolo Nega Maluca

6 servings 🕐 45 mins

This Brazilian Chocolate cake is easy and quick to prepare. A great everyday cake, that is also perfect for celebrations when topped with sweet brigadeiro.

Method

Step 1: Preheat the oven to 350F

Step 2: Spray a bundt or 11x7in sheet pan

Step 3: In a medium bowl mix in the flour, salt, baking powder, and chocolate powder, and set aside

Step 4: In a large bowl, mix in the oil and sugar, using a hand mixer, in medium speed (you can also mix by hand)

Step 5: Add the eggs one at a time, gently, mixing in low speed

Step 6: Then, add 1/3 of the dry ingredients mixture to the eggs mixture, and fold by hand with a spatula to combine. Add half of the water, and fold to combine. Add the second third of the dry ingredients, and fold to combine. Add the last of the water, and fold to combine. Add the last third of the dry ingredients, and fold to combine.

Bolo Nega Maluca

6 servings　🕐 45 mins

This Brazilian Chocolate cake is easy and quick to prepare. A great everyday cake, that is also perfect for celebrations when topped with sweet brigadeiro.

Method

Step 7: Pour the batter into the greased pan, and bake bake until a cake tester/toothpick inserted to the middle comes out lightly crumbly to clean (about 35-40 mins)

Step 8: Move the cake pan to a cooling rack and let it cool for about 10 mins, then remove the cake from the pan and let it cool in the rack

For the Brigadeiro:

Step 1: Add the condensed milk and the chocolate powder to a nonstick sauce pan and stir over medium to high heat, then keep stirring for about 10 minutes scraping the sides of the pan with a rubber spatula or wooden spoon to avoid burning. Cook until the mixture reaches 185F-195F – You can use a candy thermometer, or just a regular food thermometer to check.

Step 2: Let it cool until its cool to touch, then pour over cooled cake

Recipe 8

Portuguese Rice Pudding

8 servings   🕐 1 hr 10mins

Arroz Doce is a Portuguese rice pudding that is thick, creamy, sweet and served semi-set with a generous sprinkling of cinnamon.

Ingredients

500 g (2½ cups) arborio rice

2 pint (3½ cups) boiling water

1 lemon zest

2 pint (3½ cups) whole milk

400 g (2¼ cups) granulated white sugar

1 pinch salt

8 medium free range egg yolks

1 tbsp cinnamon

Equipment

Weighing scales

Measuring jug

Kitchen knife

Chopping board

Large saucepan

Sieve

Wooden spoon

Whisk

Ladle

Large platter

Portuguese Rice Pudding

8 servings 🕐 1 hr 10mins

Arroz Doce is a Portuguese rice pudding that is thick, creamy, sweet and served semi-set with a generous sprinkling of cinnamon.

Method

Step 1: Put the rice and lemon zest in a large pan.

Step 2: Cover with the boiling water and bring up to the boil.

Step 3: Cover and simmer for 10 minutes.

Step 4: Strain off the excess liquid through a sieve, then return the rice to the pan and add the milk.

Step 5: Heat on medium-low until bubbling, then stir in the sugar and salt. Bring almost up to the boil, then reduce to a low simmer and cook without the lid this time, stirring very regularly for about 10 minutes.

Step 6: Whisk your egg yolks with a few spoonfuls of the rice so that it doesn't scramble.

Step 7: Stir the eggs into the pot.

Portuguese Rice Pudding

8 servings 🕐 1 hr 10mins

Arroz Doce is a Portuguese rice pudding that is thick, creamy, sweet and served semi-set with a generous sprinkling of cinnamon.

Method

Step 8: Now it's a game of patience, keep heating and it will thicken - remember to stir well every now and then so that it doesn't burn. After 30-40 minutes you'll have lovely thick, creamy rice pudding

Step 9: When you think it's thick enough, pick some up on your spoon and let it drop. If it briefly holds its shape before dolloping off the spoon, it's thick enough and will thicken more as it cools!

Step 10: Ladle your pudding onto a large platter and leave to set for a few minutes.

Step 11: Using a pinched thumb and forefinger, carefully sprinkle on your crosshatch cinnamon pattern, or any design you fancy.

Step 12: Once completely cooled, the pudding will have firmed up enough to serve by the spoonful. DIVINE!

Recipe 9

Honey Cake

10 servings   🕐 2 hrs 50mins

This delicious and moist honey cake recipe, with a tangy sour cream frosting and prominent honey flavor, is a cake that will take a very special place in your heart. It's a great dessert to make for any occasion, whether it's New Year's, a birthday, or even a wedding.

Ingredients

For the cake layers:

- 2 large eggs at room temperature
- 120 g unsalted butter
- 80 g granulated sugar
- 140 g honey
- 10 g baking soda
- 420 g all-purpose flour
- ½ teaspoon salt

For the cream:

- 600 g full-fat sour cream such as from Daisy (cold)
- 160 ml heavy whipping cream cold
- 100 g powdered sugar
- 3 tablespoon honey
- Fresh raspberries for decoration

Honey Cake

10 servings   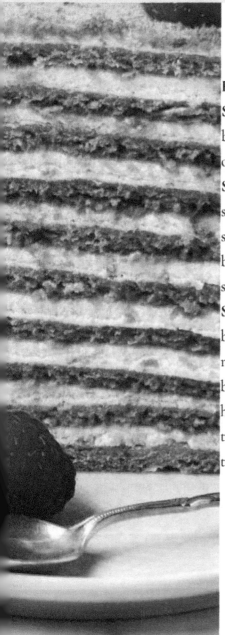 2 hrs 50mins

This delicious and moist honey cake recipe, with a tangy sour cream frosting and prominent honey flavor, is a cake that will take a very special place in your heart. It's a great dessert to make for any occasion, whether it's New Year's, a birthday, or even a wedding.

Method

For the cake layers

Step 1: Whip the eggs in a large mixing bowl with a hand mixer for one minute or until pale. Set aside.

Step 2: In a heavy-bottomed medium saucepan, add the butter, honey, and sugar. Heat over medium heat until the butter has melted and the mixture starts simmering.

Step 3: Lower the heat to low and add baking soda. Whisk to combine. The mixture will bubble and expand a lot but will then subside. Cook over low heat, stirring continuously to prevent the honey burning, until the mixture turns a light amber color.

Honey Cake

10 servings   🕐 2 hrs 50mins

This delicious and moist honey cake recipe, with a tangy sour cream frosting and prominent honey flavor, is ... cake that will take a very special place in your heart. It's a great dessert to make for any occasion, whether it ... New Year's, a birthday, or even a wedding.

Method

Step 4: Remove from the heat and slowly pour the honey mixture into the eggs, whisking vigorously. Then, sift in the flour with salt and mix until no dry ingredients are left. The dough should be sticky, don't add more flour! Wrap the dough in plastic wrap and place it in the fridge for 1 hour.

Step 5: Preheat the oven to 180C (355F). Prepare a baking sheet and 10 pieces of parchment paper (one for each cake layer).

Step 6: Split the dough into 10 even parts (around 85g each). Take one piece and place it on parchment paper, cover it with a piece of plastic wrap, and roll the dough (it should be 1-2mm thick) you can cut out a 7"/17cm disc and have some left over.

Honey Cake

10 servings 🕐 2 hrs 50mins

This delicious and moist honey cake recipe, with a tangy sour cream frosting and prominent honey flavor, is a cake that will take a very special place in your heart. It's a great dessert to make for any occasion, whether it's New Year's, a birthday, or even a wedding.

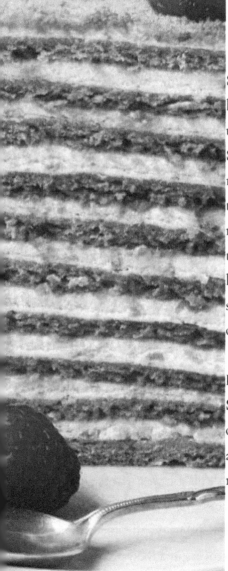

Method

Step 7: Cut out a 7" disc and spread the leftovers 1 inch away from it. We will use the leftovers to decorate the cake.

Step 8: Bake each layer for around 4 minutes or until golden. Remove from the oven and let it cool down for a minute on the baking sheet. Then, transfer it onto a cooling rack. Place the leftovers onto a separate plate. Don't stack baked cake layers on top of each other if they're still warm.

For the cream
Step 1: Place all ingredients in the bowl of a stand mixer fitted with a whisk attachment (or use a bowl and a hand mixer).

47

Honey Cake

10 servings   ⏱ 2 hrs 50mins

This delicious and moist honey cake recipe, with a tangy sour cream frosting and prominent honey flavor, is a cake that will take a very special place in your heart. It's a great dessert to make for any occasion, whether it's New Year's, a birthday, or even a wedding.

Method

Step 2: Whip to stiff peaks (3-4 minutes on medium-high), scraping the sides and the bottom of the bowl couple of times in between.

Assembling the cake

Step 1: Spread one teaspoon of the cream on the surface/plate that you're going to use to assemble your cake.

Step 2: Place the first cake layer on top. Then, add around ⅔ cup (80g) of the cream and spread it evenly. Cover with the second cake layer and repeat the process until no cake layers are left.

Step 3: Crumb coat the cake with the rest of the cream and cover the cake with plastic wrap. Refrigerate for 2 hours.

Step 4: Meanwhile, place the cake layer leftovers in a food processor and pulse until a fine crumb is reached.

Honey Cake

10 servings 🕐 2 hrs 50mins

This delicious and moist honey cake recipe, with a tangy sour cream frosting and prominent honey flavor, is a cake that will take a very special place in your heart. It's a great dessert to make for any occasion, whether it's New Year's, a birthday, or even a wedding.

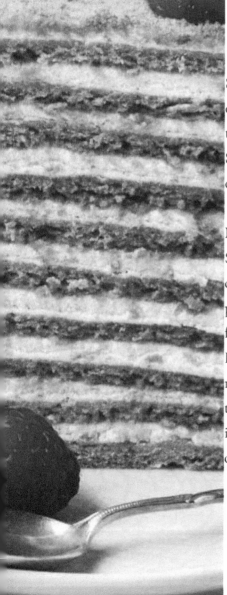

Method

Step 5: When the cake is chilled, dust it evenly with the crumbs and decorate the top with fresh berries.

Step 6: The cake is best served the next day.

Notes

Store the cake in a plastic cake container (or you can place it on a large plate covered with plastic wrap) in the fridge for up to 4 days.

Freeze the cake dough for up to 2 months. Wrap it in a plastic wrap and then in a piece of foil and freeze. Thaw in the fridge overnight before rolling it out and baking.

Honey Cake

10 servings   🕐 2 hrs 50mins

This delicious and moist honey cake recipe, with a tangy sour cream frosting and prominent honey flavor, is a cake that will take a very special place in your heart. It's a great dessert to make for any occasion, whether it's New Year's, a birthday, or even a wedding.

Method

Step 5: When the cake is chilled, dust it evenly with the crumbs and decorate the top with fresh berries.

Step 6: The cake is best served the next day.

Notes

Store the cake in a plastic cake container (or you can place it on a large plate covered with plastic wrap) in the fridge for up to 4 days.

Freeze the cake dough for up to 2 months. Wrap it in a plastic wrap and then in a piece of foil and freeze. Thaw in the fridge overnight before rolling it out and baking.

Recipe 10

Bolo Rei

6 servings   🕐 2 hrs 25mins

A lightly spiced, fluffy Christmas cake filled with fruit and nuts. A speciality in Portugal, Bolo Rei or Portuguese Kings Cake, is super easy to bake at home, so get ready to make your Kings Cake "crown" this holiday season!

Ingredients

3 cups plain flour / all purpose flour

2 tbsp dried yeast

1/2 cup sugar

75 g butter softened

2 eggs

1 egg whisked – for basting

Pinch salt

lemon zest from 1 lemon

100 ml warm milk

100 ml port wine or brandy or sweet sherry

80 g candied or dried fruit chopped fo filling, sultanas okay

50 g mixed nuts unsalted and choppec (walnuts, almonds, pine nuts)

Garnish

50 g dried fruit slices

30 g mixed nuts unsalted and halved (walnuts, almonds, pine nuts)

Sprinkle icing sugar / powdered sugar

1 tsp strawberry jam (jelly)

2 tsp hot water

Bolo Rei

6 servings   🕐 2 hrs 25mins

A lightly spiced, fluffy Christmas cake filled with fruit and nuts. A speciality in Portugal, Bolo Rei or Portuguese Kings Cake, is super easy to bake at home, so get ready to make your Kings Cake "crown" this holiday season!

Method

Step 1: Place the chopped candied fruit and raisins in a bowl with the port to infuse.

100 ml port wine,80 g candied or dried fruit

Step 2: Mix the yeast with warm milk and let rest in a warm place for 5-10 minutes until slightly frothy on top.

2 tbsp dried yeast,100 ml warm milk

Step 3: In a large bowl, mix the flour, sugar, lemon zest, butter, whole eggs and salt. Then pour in the yeast milk and knead together.

3 cups plain flour / all purpose flour, 75 g butter, 2 eggs, Pinch salt, lemon zest,1/2 cup sugar

Step 4: Once mixed, add in the port and fruits mixture and the chopped nuts. Knead together until well combined.

50 g mixed nuts

Bolo Rei

6 servings   🕐 2 hrs 25mins

A lightly spiced, fluffy Christmas cake filled with fruit and nuts. A speciality in Portugal, Bolo Rei or Portuguese Kings Cake, is super easy to bake at home, so get ready to make your Kings Cake "crown" this holiday season!

Method

Step 5: Mould the dough to be rounded or in a ball shape within the bowl, scraping down the edges and slightly sprinkle with flour before covering it over with cling wrap and a cloth. Allow to rise to double the size. This should take around 1.5 hours, depending on your climate.

Step 6: Line a baking tray with paper and a light sprinkling of flour. Place the dough onto the tray, forming a ring or "crown", without handling the dough too much. Place a cup or dish in the centre to keep the ring from closing up. Allow to rise for another 30min – 1 hour.

Step 7: Preheat oven to 180°c.

Bolo Rei

6 servings   🕐 2 hrs 25mins

A lightly spiced, fluffy Christmas cake filled with fruit and nuts. A speciality in Portugal, Bolo Rei or Portuguese Kings Cake, is super easy to bake at home, so get ready to make your Kings Cake "crown" this holiday season!

Method

Step 8: Baste with whisked egg and garnish with remaining nuts, dried fruit slices and icing sugar.

1 egg,50 g dried fruit slices, Sprinkle icing sugar / powdered sugar,30 g mixed nuts

Step 9: Pop in the oven and bake for 35 to 45 minutes.

Step 10:

Optional: Brush the top with the jam and hot water mix to add a finishing shine before serving.

1 tsp strawberry jam,2 tsp hot water

Recipe 11

Orange Sweet Rolls

15 servings   🕐 3 hrs

With one taste of the warm and sticky rolls fresh from the oven, I truly wondered why I waited so long to make these! I like to unravel the doughy cinnamon layers as I eat them.

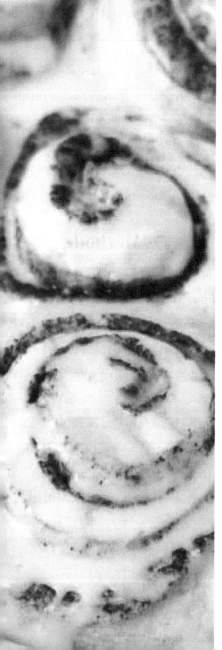

Ingredients

Dough

- 1 package active dry yeast (2 and 1/4 teaspoons)
- 1/2 cup warm water
- fresh orange zest from 1 medium orange
- 1/2 cup orange juice
- 1/4 cup granulated sugar
- 1 teaspoon salt
- 1 large egg
- 2 Tablespoons unsalted butter, softened to room temperature
- 3 – 3 and 1/2 cups all-purpose flour (spoon & leveled)

Filling

- 1/4 cup granulated sugar
- 2 teaspoons ground cinnamon
- 1/4 cup unsalted butter, softened to room temperature

Orange Sweet Rolls

15 servings 🕐 3 hrs

With one taste of the warm and sticky rolls fresh from the oven, I truly wondered why I waited so long to make these! I like to unravel the doughy cinnamon layers as I eat them.

Ingredients

Glaze

- 1 cup confectioners' sugar (or mor for a thicker glaze)
- 3 Tablespoons orange juice
- fresh orange zest from 1 orange
- 1 teaspoon pure vanilla extract

Method

Step 1: Make the dough: Dissolve the yeast in 1/2 cup warm water for about minute. No need to use a thermometer for the water's temperature, but to be precise: about 105°F (41°C)-115°F (46°C Stir the yeast/water around. Then add orange zest, orange juice, sugar, salt, eg butter, and 1.5 cups of flour. Beat everything together on low with a handheld mixer, scraping down the sic as needed.

Orange Sweet Rolls

15 servings 3 hrs

With one taste of the warm and sticky rolls fresh from the oven, I truly wondered why I waited so long to make these! I like to unravel the doughy cinnamon layers as I eat them.

Method

(A mixer is definitely needed to break up all the butter and beat everything to the proper consistency.) With a wooden spoon, stir in enough of the remaining flour to make a dough easy to handle – about 1.5 – 2 more cups. You are looking for a dough that is not sticky and will spring back when poked with a finger.

Step 2: Transfer the dough to a lightly floured surface and knead it with your hands for about 5-6 minutes. Form the dough into a ball and transfer it to a lightly greased bowl. Cover the dough and let sit in a warm place until doubled in size, about 1.5 hours.

Orange Sweet Rolls

15 servings   🕐 3 hrs

With one taste of the warm and sticky rolls fresh from the oven, I truly wondered why I waited so long to make these! I like to unravel the doughy cinnamon layers as I eat them.

Method

Step 3: Line the bottom of a 9×13 inch baking dish with parchment paper, leaving room on the sides. Turn the dough out onto a lightly floured work surface and, using a rolling in, roll into a 10×15 inch rectangle. I used a ruler for accuracy. Make sure the dough is smooth and evenly thick, even at the corners.

Step 4: For the filling: in a small bowl, mix together sugar and cinnamon. Spread the dough rectangle with softened butter and sprinkle generousl with all of the cinnamon-sugar mixture Tightly roll up the dough and cut into 16 even rolls (1 inch in width each) with a very sharp knife. Arrange them in the prepared baking pan, cut sides up.

Step 5: Cover the rolls and let them ris in a warm place for about 30 minutes - 1 hour.

Orange Sweet Rolls

15 servings   🕐 3 hrs

With one taste of the warm and sticky rolls fresh from the oven, I truly wondered why I waited so long to make these! I like to unravel the doughy cinnamon layers as I eat them.

Method

Step 6: Preheat the oven to 375°F (191°C). Cover the rolls with aluminum foil and bake for about 25-30 minutes, until they are lightly golden in color. Transfer the pan to a rack to cool for about 15 minutes.

Step 7: Make the glaze: In a small bowl, mix together all of the glaze ingredients and drizzle over rolls before serving. Add more orange juice to thin out, if needed.

Recipe 12

Caramelized Apple Cake

8 servings   🕐 1 hr 30 mins

This stunning apple upside down cake combines a soft cinnamon-spiced cake with a delicious buttery caramel topping. Pack those apples into the pan—this cake can hold a lot and you won't regret those extra slices!

Ingredients

Topping

- 6 Tablespoons (85g) unsalted butter
- 1/2 cup (100g) packed light or dark brown sugar
- 1/4 teaspoon ground cinnamon
- 1/4 teaspoon pure vanilla extract
- 2 medium apples, peeled and sliced into 1/4-inch slices (1.5–2 cups, or 188–250g, apple slices)*

Cake

- 1 and 1/2 cups (188g) all-purpose flour (spooned & leveled)
- 1 and 1/2 teaspoons baking powder
- 1 and 1/2 teaspoons ground cinnamon
- 1/4 teaspoon ground nutmeg
- 1/2 teaspoon salt
- 1/2 cup (8 Tbsp; 113g) unsalted butter, softened to room temperature

Caramelized Apple Cake

8 servings 1 hr 30 mins

This stunning apple upside down cake combines a soft cinnamon-spiced cake with a delicious buttery carame *topping. Pack those apples into the pan—this cake can hold a lot and you won't regret those extra slices!*

Ingredients

- 1/2 cup (100g) granulated sugar
- 1/2 cup (100g) packed light or dark brown sugar
- 2 large eggs, at room temperature
- 1 teaspoon pure vanilla extract
- 6 Tablespoons (90ml) whole milk. at room temperature*

Method

Step 1: Preheat oven to 350°F (177°C).
Step 2: Prepare topping first: Combin butter and brown sugar together in a small saucepan over medium heat. Whisk occasionally until butter has melted. Cook, whisking constantly, fc 1 minute as mixture thickens. Remove from heat and whisk in the cinnamon and vanilla extract.

Caramelized Apple Cake

8 servings   🕐 1 hr 30 mins

This stunning apple upside down cake combines a soft cinnamon-spiced cake with a delicious buttery caramel topping. Pack those apples into the pan—this cake can hold a lot and you won't regret those extra slices!

Method

Pour into an ungreased 9×2 inch pie dish or round cake pan. (Make sure the pan is 2 inches deep. I recommend this pie dish, which is 1.8 inches deep but I never have an overflow issue.) Arrange the apple slices neatly on top, overlapping where necessary. Place pan in the refrigerator for a few minutes as you prepare the cake batter. This helps solidify or "set" the topping's arrangement.

Step 3: Make the cake batter: Whisk the flour, baking powder, cinnamon, nutmeg, and salt together. Set aside.

Step 4: Using a handheld or stand mixer fitted with a paddle or whisk attachment, beat the butter on high speed until smooth and creamy, about 1 minute. Add both sugars and beat on high speed until creamed together, about 1 minute.

Caramelized Apple Cake

8 servings   🕐 1 hr 30 mins

This stunning apple upside down cake combines a soft cinnamon-spiced cake with a delicious buttery caramel topping. Pack those apples into the pan—this cake can hold a lot and you won't regret those extra slices!

Method

Scrape down the sides and up the bottom of the bowl with a rubber spatula as needed. On high speed, beat in the eggs and vanilla extract until combined. Scrape down the sides and up the bottom of the bowl as needed. Pour the dry ingredients into the wet ingredients. Turn the mixer onto low speed and as the mixer runs, slowly pour in the milk. Beat on low speed just until all of the ingredients are combined. Do not over-mix. You may need to whisk it all by hand to make sure there are no lumps at the bottom of the bowl. The batter will be slightly thick.

Step 5: Remove topping from the refrigerator. Pour and spread cake batter evenly over topping.

Caramelized Apple Cake

8 servings 🕐 1 hr 30 mins

This stunning apple upside down cake combines a soft cinnamon-spiced cake with a delicious buttery caramel topping. Pack those apples into the pan—this cake can hold a lot and you won't regret those extra slices!

Method

Step 6: Bake for 40-46 minutes, tenting foil on top of the cake halfway through bake time to prevent the top from over-browning before the center has a chance to fully cook. The cake is done when a toothpick inserted into the center of the cake comes out mostly clean– a couple moist crumbs are OK. Don't be alarmed if your cake takes longer or if the cake rises up and sticks to the foil. (We serve the cake upside down anyway!)

Step 7: Remove cake from the oven and cool on a wire rack for just 15 minutes. Invert the slightly cooled cake onto a cake stand or serving plate. Some of the juices from the topping will seep over the sides– that's ok. You can slice and serve the cake warm, but the slices will be messy. I find it's best to cool the cake completely at room temperature before slicing and serving.

67

Caramelized Apple Cake

8 servings 🕐 1 hr 30 mins

This stunning apple upside down cake combines a soft cinnamon-spiced cake with a delicious buttery caramel topping. Pack those apples into the pan—this cake can hold a lot and you won't regret those extra slices!

Method

Do not refrigerate the cake to speed up the cooling process because it could end up tasting overly dense.

Step 8: Cover leftover slices and store for up to 3 days in the refrigerator or 3 months in the freezer. Thaw at room temperature. I don't recommend freezing the cake as a whole because the topping arrangement doesn't thaw very nicely.

Recipe 13

Classic Caramel Flan

6 servings   🕐 1 hr 10 mins (cook) + 8hrs (passive)

This stunning apple upside down cake combines a soft cinnamon-spiced cake with a delicious buttery caramel topping. Pack those apples into the pan—this cake can hold a lot and you won't regret those extra slices!

Ingredients

The Caramel

- 1 cup sugar (200 g)
- ¼ cup water (60 ml)
- 1 ½ teaspoon lemon juice

The Creme Custard

- 2 cup full fat milk (500 ml), room temperature
- 4 eggs , room temperature
- 14 oz sweetened condensed milk (400 g)
- 1 tablespoon vanilla extract

Classic Caramel Flan

6 servings   🕐 1 hr 10 mins (cook) + 8hrs (passive)

This stunning apple upside down cake combines a soft cinnamon-spiced cake with a delicious buttery caramel topping. Pack those apples into the pan—this cake can hold a lot and you won't regret those extra slices!

Method

The Caramel

Step 1: Add all caramel ingredients in a pot and cook on medium heat, untouched, until it turns amber color.

Step 2: Carefully divide the caramel into 6x1 cup (250 ml) container. Holding the tip of the container, carefully swirl so that the caramel coats ½ way the inner wall of the container. Set aside.

The Creme Custard

Step 1: Into a bowl, add in eggs, condensed milk and vanilla extract. Use a hand whisk and gently mix everything together.

Step 2: Then pour in milk into the eggs mixture. Again, gently mix everything. Sift the mixture to discard any lumps. Pour into prepared containers, leaving a bit less than ½ inch (1.3 cm) space to the brim.

Classic Caramel Flan

6 servings   🕐   1 hr 10 mins (cook) + 8hrs (passive)

This stunning apple upside down cake combines a soft cinnamon-spiced cake with a delicious buttery caramel topping. Pack those apples into the pan—this cake can hold a lot and you won't regret those extra slices!

Method

Step 3: Cover each container with aluminium foil and then place them in deep baking tray. Pour hot water until ½ way of the baking tray, using bain-marie method.

Step 4: Bake in preheated oven at 280°F (140°C) for 60 minutes or until cooked and set yet still wiggly. Remove from the hot water and leave to cool to room temperature. Then chill in the fridge overnight or minimum 8 hours.

Notes

- *How To Get Silky Smooth Texture:* Don't over-whisk the mixture or whisk it harshly. Always mix gently. Over-whisking will incorporate air inside the mixture, creating bubbles when cooked. Always use a low temperature.

Classic Caramel Flan

6 servings 🕐 1 hr 10 mins (cook) + 8hrs (passive)

This stunning apple upside down cake combines a soft cinnamon-spiced cake with a delicious buttery caramel topping. Pack those apples into the pan—this cake can hold a lot and you won't regret those extra slices!

Method

- *How To Know When Creme Caramel Is Cooked:*

Check after minute 30 of cooking time by gently inserting a knife inside the creme caramel mixture. If it comes out clean, then it's cooked.

If it's not clean, keep checking every 10 minutes after that.

Recipe 14

Checkerboard Cake

12 servings   🕐 6hrs 25mins

A checkerboard cake is impressive and surprisingly easy to make. Four layers of vanilla and chocolate cake frosted with chocolate ganache create this wonderful checkerboard effect. A fun new way to decorate a cake!

Ingredients

Vanilla cake batter

- 4 cups (500 g) All-purpose flour
- 2 tsp Baking powder
- 1 tsp Baking Soda
- ½ tsp Salt
- 1 ½ cup (340 g) Unsalted Butter (unsalted, room temperature)
- 2 cups (400 g) Sugar (granulated)
- ⅓ cup (80 ml) Cooking oil
- 5 large Eggs
- 2 tsp Vanilla extract
- 2 cups (470 ml) Sour cream

Chocolate cake batter

- ¼ cup (20 g) Cocoa powder
- ¼ cup (60 ml) Hot water
- 1 tsp Coffee powder (instant)

Chocolate ganache

- 1 lb (450 g) Chocolate (semi-sweet or dark)
- 1½ cup (350 ml) Whipping cream (38% fat)
- 1 tsp Vanilla extract

Checkerboard Cake

12 servings   6hrs 25mins

A checkerboard cake is impressive and surprisingly easy to make. Four layers of vanilla and chocolate cake frosted with chocolate ganache create this wonderful checkerboard effect. A fun new way to decorate a cake!

Method

Cake batter

Step 1: Oven – Preheat the oven to 325°F 165°C/ Gas Mark 3

Step 2: Pans – Grease and line with parchment paper 7-inch pans 4 x 7-inch round cake pans or 3 x 8-inch round cake pans.

Step 3: Chocolate paste – combine th hot water, cocoa powder, and coffee powder to make a thick chocolate pas Set aside to cool while you prepare th batter.

¼ cup Cocoa powder, 1 tsp Coffee powder, ¼ cup Hot water

Step 4: Dry ingredients – Sift togethe flour, baking powder, baking soda, ai salt, Set aside.

4 cups All-purpose flour, 2 tsp Baking powder, 1 tsp Baking Soda, ½ tsp Salt

Checkerboard Cake

12 servings   🕐 6hrs 25mins

A checkerboard cake is impressive and surprisingly easy to make. Four layers of vanilla and chocolate cake frosted with chocolate ganache create this wonderful checkerboard effect. A fun new way to decorate a cake!

Method

Step 5: Wet ingredients – In a bowl of a stand mixer with the paddle attachment on medium speed, cream together butter and sugar until light and fluffy. Then, gradually add the oil followed by the eggs one at a time and the vanilla extract.

Pro tip – add the eggs one at a time making sure each is well incorporated to prevent it from separating.

1 ½ cup Unsalted Butter,2 cups Sugar,⅓ cup Cooking oil,5 large Eggs,2 tsp Vanilla extract

Step 6: Combine – Next, add the flour mixture and sour cream in three batches making sure to combine well but do not overmix. This will be a thick drop consistency batter so do not add more milk or water unless necessary.

2 cups Sour cream

Checkerboard Cake

12 servings   🕐 6hrs 25mins

A checkerboard cake is impressive and surprisingly easy to make. Four layers of vanilla and chocolate cake frosted with chocolate ganache create this wonderful checkerboard effect. A fun new way to decorate a cake!

Method

Step 7: Divide – Using two similar size bowls divide the batter into two portions. One for the vanilla and one for the chocolate.

Pro tip – I like to use two similar bowl and divide the batter approximately. Alternatively, you can also use a scale s I have two equal portions.

Step 8: Vanilla batter – Nothing needs to be done. Divide the vanilla batter between the two prepared baking pans (2 vanilla cake layers)

Step 9: Chocolate batter – Add the chocolate paste mixture to the second batter. Then divide this batter betwee the other two prepared baking pans. (2 chocolate cake layers)

Step 10: Bake – Transfer the pans to th oven and bake for about 25 to 30 minutes or until a toothpick inserted i the center of the cake comes out clean

Checkerboard Cake

12 servings   🕐 6hrs 25mins

A checkerboard cake is impressive and surprisingly easy to make. Four layers of vanilla and chocolate cake frosted with chocolate ganache create this wonderful checkerboard effect. A fun new way to decorate a cake!

Method

Pro tip – if necessary rotate the pans in the oven halfway through the baking.

Step 11: Cool – When baked cool in the pan for 10 minutes then invert on a cooling rack and cool completely. At least a few hours before frosting

Pro tip – I prefer to let the cakes cool overnight. Frosting warm cakes will cause the frosting to melt.

Frosting

Step 1: Chocolate ganache – In a microwave-safe bowl, heat the chocolate and cream until melted and smooth. Let cool at room temperature overnight or for a few hours in the fridge until set. You want the ganache to set to about peanut consistency.

Checkerboard Cake

12 servings   🕐 6hrs 25mins

A checkerboard cake is impressive and surprisingly easy to make. Four layers of vanilla and chocolate cake frosted with chocolate ganache create this wonderful checkerboard effect. A fun new way to decorate a cake!

Method

Pro tip – Alternatively you can heat the heavy cream in a saucepan and pour hot cream over the chocolate. Stir until smooth. Then cool until thick.
1 lb Chocolate,1½ cup Whipping cream,1 tsp Vanilla extract

Step 2: Whipped chocolate ganache – Whip the chilled ganache in a stand mixer with the whisk attachment until light and fluffy. DO NOT OVERWHIP.

Pro tip – Overwhiped ganache will become hard. If that happens add one or two tablespoons of hot milk and whip until smooth.

Checkboard cake

Step 1: Level – Once cooled, use a bread knife to cut the domes off the cake layers.

Checkerboard Cake

12 servings   🕐 6hrs 25mins

A checkerboard cake is impressive and surprisingly easy to make. Four layers of vanilla and chocolate cake frosted with chocolate ganache create this wonderful checkerboard effect. A fun new way to decorate a cake!

Method

Step 2: Cut the circles – For the 7-inch cakes, I used a 5-inch and a 2½-inch cookie cutter.

– Using the cookie cutter cut each cake layer into 3 rings as shown in the video.

– Do that with all four cakes.

Pro tip – you can also use a small plate, bowl, glass, etc. as a guide to cut the cake into even rings.

Step 3: Arrange the circles

Rearrange the cake rings so you have chocolate and vanilla in each cake as shown in the video.

Now, do the same with all until you have 4 similar cakes with alternate colors.

Pro tip – it is easier to work with two cakes at a time so you can interchange the rings without confusion.

Checkerboard Cake

12 servings   🕐 6hrs 25mins

A checkerboard cake is impressive and surprisingly easy to make. Four layers of vanilla and chocolate cake frosted with chocolate ganache create this wonderful checkerboard effect. A fun new way to decorate a cake!

Method

Assemble

Step 1: Simple syrup – Brush each laye with the cooled simple syrup.

Pro tip – simple syrup is sugar boiled water until melted and cooled. It help keep the cakes moist.

Step 2: Stack – Place a cake layer on t cake board or cake stand. Top with a big dollop of ganache spread evenly using a straight-edge spatula. Top the second cake layer on top followed by more ganache until you have used up the cake layers.

Step 3: Crumb coat – Spread more ganache on the top and sides of the c with a spatula. Then, place the cake i the fridge for 15 minutes this will prevent the layers from moving while you frost the outside of the cake.

Checkerboard Cake

12 servings 🕐 6hrs 25mins

A checkerboard cake is impressive and surprisingly easy to make. Four layers of vanilla and chocolate cake frosted with chocolate ganache create this wonderful checkerboard effect. A fun new way to decorate a cake!

Method

Step 4: Frost – When chilled spread more ganache around and on the top of the cake. Use a cake bench scraper to smooth the sides and an offset spatula for the top. Smooth with a bench scraper as best you can.

Step 5: Borders – Put any remaining frosting in a piping bag and pipe a border around the cake as well as on top of the cake.

Step 6: Garnish with chocolate decorations as desired.

~~~ Recipe 15 ~~~

Bolos de Arroz

6 servings   🕐 45 mins

A traditional Portuguese muffin made with part rice flour, which gives the muffins a tender crumb with a buttery flavor and a hint of lemon, and a delightful crunchy sugar crust on top.

Ingredients

- ¾ cup / 150 g granulated sugar, plus more for topping
- ⅓ cup / 75 g unsalted butter, at room temperature
- 2 ½ teaspoons / 11 g baking powder
- 1 teaspoon lemon zest
- Pinch kosher salt
- 3 large eggs, at room temperature
- scant ½ cup / 100 ml whole milk, more or less as needed
- 1 cup / 125 g all-purpose flour
- ⅔ cup / 100 g rice flour

Bolos de Arroz

6 servings   🕐 45 mins

A traditional Portuguese muffin made with part rice flour, which gives the muffins a tender crumb with a buttery flavor and a hint of lemon, and a delightful crunchy sugar crust on top.

Method

Step 1: Preheat oven to 400 degrees F. Arrange 6 paper baking molds on a silicone-lined baking sheet (it will help keep the molds from sliding around). You can also use a jumbo or regular muffin tin, either lined with baking papers or lightly buttered.

Step 2: In a mixing bowl or the bowl of a stand mixer fitted with the paddle attachment, cream together sugar, butter, baking powder, lemon zest and salt until very light and fluffy, 5 to 6 minutes.

Step 3: Crack eggs in to a liquid measuring cup. Add enough milk to equal 250mL of liquid (this should be about 100ml, but depending on the siz of your eggs may be more or less). Whisk until mostly blended.

Bolos de Arroz

6 servings   🕐 45 mins

A traditional Portuguese muffin made with part rice flour, which gives the muffins a tender crumb with a buttery flavor and a hint of lemon, and a delightful crunchy sugar crust on top.

Method

Step 4: In a bowl, whisk together flour and rice flour until evenly incorporated.

Step 5: With the mixer on low, add about 1/3 of egg mixture. Increase the speed and beat until completely emulsified into the batter before addding another 1/3 of the liquid. Scrape down the bowl as needed. Repeat, mixing until completely incorporated before adding remaining liquid.

Step 6: Add flour and mix on low speed for a few seconds just to moisten it, then increase to high for just a few seconds until light and creamy. You obviously don't want to beat it too much, but unlike standard cake the rice flour will prevent excess gluten from forming. This final high speed mix will help bring the batter together and produce a finely textured muffin.

Bolos de Arroz

6 servings   🕐 45 mins

A traditional Portuguese muffin made with part rice flour, which gives the muffins a tender crumb with a buttery flavor and a hint of lemon, and a delightful crunchy sugar crust on top.

Method

Step 7: Divide batter among baking molds; you'll want 100 grams of batte[r] about 2 large cookie scoops worth, pe[r] muffin. For standard size muffins use single scoop or 50 grams worth. Generously sprinkle tops with granulated sugar.

Step 8: Bake for about 18 minutes or until top is crackly and barely startin[g] to brown; a toothpick inserted near t[he] center will come out mostly clean.

Step 9: Remove from oven and let co[ol] slightly; serve warm or at room temperature. Muffins are best enjoye[d] the day they are made, but can be stored in an airtight container for 1-2 days (though you will lose the crunch[] on top).